EFFECTIVENESS OF READING RECALL

A Comparative Study

Authors

Dr. Taj Mohammad
Asst. Professor, Department of English, Najran University, KSA

Dr. Soada Idris
Asst. Professor, Department of English, Najran University, KSA

AkiNik Publications
New Delhi

Published By: *AkiNik Publications*

AkiNik Publications
169, C-11, Sector - 3,
Rohini, Delhi-110085, India
Toll Free (India) – 18001234070

Authors: *Dr. Taj Mohammad and Dr. Soada Idris*

The author/publisher has attempted to trace and acknowledge the materials reproduced in this publication and apologize if permission and acknowledgements to publish in this form have not been given. If any material has not been acknowledged please write and let us know so that we may rectify it.

1st Edition: *2018*

Pages: *67*

ISBN: *978-93-5335-054-3*

Price: *₹365/-*

Preface

It is observed that reading is a cumbersome and difficult skill for readers. The reason may be attributed to the reluctance of the readers. They hardly appreciate a variety of reading subsequently resulting into selected pieces of reading catering to individual interests. However, in an academic environment, readers, especially learners, have to inevitably read various subjects to score well in the examination. Of course, many of the subjects do not suit to the interest of readers yet they have to exhaustively go through them. This book specially addresses these issues and comprehensively attempts to provide solutions. It describes several techniques like skimming, scanning, intensive, extensive etc. which in turn will assist readers to reduce time on reading materials and score better grades. In addition, the book also envisages describing several approaches to reading also like bottom-up, top-down, interactive, and global etc. This book in general deals with reading approaches, reading process and in particular deals with 'effectiveness of reading recall', a technique used in reading comprehension. The book has been divided into five chapters:

Chapter 1 focuses on statement of intent and layout of the study. It describes how readers feel different kinds of problems while reading a text. It implicitly focuses on the need of this book.

Chapter 2 deals with the reading comprehension and the state of art. It attempts to deal with the purposes and researches in reading. It also aims at processes of reading looking at the metacognition, and understanding text structure. The different approaches to reading-- bottom-up, top-down, interactive, and global have also been discussed here.

Chapter 3 attempts a review of some of the studies and researches on 'Recall in Reading' done by various researchers and scholars.

Chapter 4 contains the empirical study conducted at the +2 level, in A.M.U., Aligarh, India. It deals with the methodology, analysis and result of recall among this group of learners.

Chapter 5 concludes the results and findings of the study, highlighting the causes and effects of recall, among the students. It attempts to describe and suggest the reasons for the differences of recall among both the group of learners: boys and girls.

The book is peculiar in the sense that it not only offers theoretical basis of 'reading recall' rather it shares an action research conducted on boys and girls studying at intermediate level at Aligarh Muslim University, Aligarh. The study analyses and provides a comparative study of the gender differences related to the effectiveness of 'reading recall'.

Acknowledgement

This book is based on a research conducted at Senior Secondary School (Boys and Girls) at AMU, Aligarh, India as part of a project for master degree which subsequently went through several changes and modifications to be published as a book. We are extremely thankful to our teachers Professor Raashid Nehal and Professor M. Asim Siddiqui for their valuable inputs and suggestions while finalizing the book.

We are also very thankful to our esteemed teacher Prof. A.R. Kidwai for providing feedback on this book. This book was not possible without his valuable comments on different sections of the book.

We are also very thankful to our senior Dr. Mohammad Nazim to spare time to revise some of the sections of the book. His suggestions were of great importance.

We feel highly obliged to the editor and entire team of AkiNik Publications New Delhi for their continuous support in editing the book, designing the cover page etc.

This book is dedicated to

Prof. Raashid Nehal

and

Prof. M. Asim Siddiqui

Contents

Chapter - 1

Statement of Intent

1.1 Statement of Intent

Reading comprehension attempts to understand a student's ability to understand a passage and answer questions based on them. Students need to read the passage so that they can identify the main idea of the passage, and appreciate certain features such as the author's tone and attitude as well as the organization of the passage, and then go back to the relevant point in the text as they attempt each question. Reading comprehension is defined as the level of understanding of any written text. The normal reading rate is 200-220 words per minute. Proficient reading depends on the ability to recognize words quickly. There are a number of ways to comprehension. Much work has been done with regard to teaching strategies in comprehension and the common ones are summarizing, monitoring and analyzing the structure of a text. The U.S. National Reading Panel in its study concluded that effective reading comprehension comprised of vocabulary knowledge, reading strategies and comprehension practices.

Therefore, reading comprehension is the process of constructing meaning from text. The goal of all reading instruction is ultimately targeted at helping a reader to comprehend the text, Reading comprehension involves at least two people: the reader and the writer. The process of comprehending involves decoding the writer's words and then using the background knowledge to construct an estimated understanding of the writer's message.

Despite the fact, that word identification is a process that results in a fairly exact outcome, the process of comprehending a text is not so exact. Different readers interpret an author's message in different ways. Comprehension is affected by reader's knowledge of the topic, knowledge of language structures, knowledge of text structures and genres, knowledge of cognitive and metacognitive strategies, their reasoning abilities, their motivation, and their level of engagement.

Reading comprehension is also affected by the quality of the reading material. The more inconsiderate (poorly organized and difficult to understand) the text, the more work will be required of a reader to comprehend the text. Students who do not have the background, abilities, or motivation to overcome the barriers presented in a text will have more difficulty in comprehending these types of texts.

Students who have trouble in learning to decode and recognize the words, often, will have difficulty with reading comprehension. Students who struggle with decoding rarely have a chance to interact with more difficult text and often learn to dislike reading. As a result, these students do not have sufficient opportunities to develop the language skills and strategies necessary for becoming proficient readers.

Readers with poorly developed language skills and strategies do not have the tools to take advantage of the obvious structures and comprehension cues that are neither part of a text nor do them have extra tools needed to overcome the barriers of a text.

The type of instruction that a student receives will also affect reading comprehension. Strategies for improving reading comprehension must be taught directly by teachers. Simply providing opportunities or requiring for children to read will not teach many students the comprehension strategies. These strategies need to be taught directly as students learn to read simple sentences and this direct instruction needs to be continued in different forms throughout a student's elementary and secondary school experience.

An important area of reading comprehension is recall which is related to memory and cognition. Studies in this area attempt to view how recall is associated with recognition and fluency and its effect on what and how much information is retrieved by a skilled learner. Studies have suggested that there is a link between knowledge of structure and recall of a passage. Repetitive listening or reading a passage has shown some correlations between the original passage and the passage produced. The nature of information recalled is also dependent on a number of factors. The recalled items were reflected in the various clausal units of a passage. The type of passage administered for recall also had an effect on the outcome. A widely used awareness measure has been the written recall which has been analyzed not only for the number of ideas recalled but also for the way in which readers use the same organizational pattern.

For this book the effects of recall of an expository text has been analyzed. The observants were the students of Arts group at the intermediate level. English was being taught to them as an optional subject of study. The intention of using listening activity was to introduce and enhance the ability of listening comprehension and ability to recall. As Karen Kow Yip Cheng

(2001) [1], [as taken from Marybeth Coleman (2002)] mentioned that by listening to stories children learn in turn to tell stories, which involves communicating meaning. Some of the benefits as he stated are

- Listening feeds the child's imagination.
- Sharpens the child's listening skills.
- Extends child's vocabulary and.
- Raises child's level of proficiency in the language.

In the composition literature, support for these activities has come largely from intuitive arguments about the value of writing as a way to learn. Emig, for example, in her seminal essay "Writing as a Mode of Learning" (1977), as mentioned in Craige (2008) [2], argued that one way in which writing helps us to learn is by forcing us to engage actively with our material. Shaughnessy (1977) [3] suggested that this activity embeds the material more "deeply" in memory. Others have described writing as a "connective" activity, arguing that the process of writing forces us to discover and articulate relationships between what might otherwise be discrete bits of knowledge and encourages us to go beyond the text, to engage in imaginative and speculative thinking (Fulwiler, 1982) [4].

We know writing can enhance students' learning in important and exciting ways, but we also know that the value of writing as a means of learning varies from one writing task to another, from one classroom to another, and from one student to the next. Research to date suggests four key variables in the relationship between writing and learning: the type of learning desired, the nature of the material to be learned, the nature of the writing task, and characteristics of writers themselves.

Studies of writing-to-learn have defined "learning" in a number of ways. The easiest type of learning for testing purposes is simple comprehension, particularly factual recall, and most experimental studies have included measures of this sort. Results on this type of learning have been mixed. When compared with non- writing activities such as answering multiple-choice questions, writing does appear to help students remember and use facts from their reading.

1.2 The Layout of Study

Chapter - 1

Statement of intent

Chapter- 2

This chapter deals with the reading comprehension and the state of art. It attempts to deal with the purposes and researches in reading It also aims at processes of reading looking at the metacognition, and understanding text structure. The different approaches to reading-- bottom-up, top-down, interactive, and global have also been discussed.

Chapter- 3

This chapter attempts a review of some of the studies and researches on 'Recall in Reading' done by different researchers and scholars.

Chapter- 4

The empirical study conducted at the +2 level, in A.M.U., has been discussed in this chapter. It deals with the methodology, analysis and result of recall among this group of learners.

Chapter- 5

This chapter concludes the results and findings of the study, highlighting the causes and effects of recall, among the students. It attempts to describe and suggest the reasons for the differences of recall among both the group of learners.

Chapter - 2

Reading Comprehension: State of Arts

2.0 Reading Comprehension: State of Arts

2.1 What is Reading?

2.1.1 Definition of Reading

Catherine Wallace [(1998) p. no. ix] [1] considers reading as a social, interactive process as much as a personal and private activity. It has to do with language. It is used for a personal and private activity. It is used for a purpose and it makes sense only in a context.

Reading is a complex process comprising many interrelated factors: language visual discrimination, auditory discrimination, memory and cognitive development [Sharma, (2006)] [2].

Reading is basically, a decoding process-a process for learning the relationship between symbols and spoken sounds. Once these associations are learned, the child is a reader. Some experts claimed that reading is **"gaining meaning from the printed page"** [Spodek, B. (1972) p. no.89] [3]. The process of interpreting the sounds associated with the letters is also a part of the reading process and needs to be included in any program of instruction. Others suggest that the reading process is really an extension of intellectual process, for interpretation of meaning. It is a significant part of reading. Critical reading, problem solving and other complex of process need to be included in any reading program. Reading is part of the language process that deals with the decoding of written symbols. It is a translation of written symbols into their equivalent sound symbols and is a linguistic process. Hence it is incomplete until meaning has been derived from the symbols [Spodek, B. (1972) p. no.89] [4].

Reading is a multifaceted process involving word recognition, comprehension, fluency, and motivation. It is meaning making process. It requires that a reader:

- Identifies the words in print – a process called word recognition
- Constructs an understanding from them -- a process called comprehension.

- Coordinates identifying words and meaning making so that reading is automatic and accurate -- an achievement called fluency [Spodek (1972) p. no. 90] [5].

Reading is not simply decoding written language to spoken language. It does not involve the processing of each letter and each word. It is a matter of bringing meaning to print, not extracting meaning from print.

2.1.2 Researches in Reading

Formerly, reading was considered to be a simple mechanical skill. Even today, some have held this concept, as they are unfamiliar with the psychology of reading act. For some it is reading aloud either with or without understanding the meaning. For others, the concept of reading is restricted to the ability of reading aloud, as their assumption is that good oral readers automatically make good silent readers. Reading is a much more complex process. Reflective reading involves all of the higher mental processes. It involves recall, reasoning, evolution, imagining, organizing and problem solving. Good reading requires good thinking. Research findings show that reading includes all perceptive and observation of the real world around us. Reading should be thought of an activity which involves the comprehension and interpretation of ideas symbolized by written or printed language [Sharma, (2006) pp. 215-234)] [6].

Salwa Ibrahim (1979)[7] [as it is mentioned in Ronald Mackay, Barkman, B. and Jordon, R. R. (1979)] stated that reading might be defined as an act of information processing. This act might be broken down as a result of so many factors: an inadequate vocabulary, inability to handle grammatical structures, failures to recognize the logical connections between sentences, incorrect utilization of context, and /or complete novelty of the material. He believed that besides the skill of recognizing the logical relationship between sentences and other basic skills of recognizing lexical and structural relationships, the total comprehension of a reading passage involves two types of skills

a. The skills to glean the ideas that the writer is discussing.
b. The skill to extract the organizational pattern the writer has used to express his ideas.

It is second skill which plays a vital role in reading comprehension because it provides the content to be read with a frame of reference.

In order to decode a specific message successfully, the reader has to subject his own logic or reasoning to that assumed by the encoder or writer and to reconstruct the logical organization he had chosen as a frame work for his message. Complete comprehension occurs when the recipient of a message becomes aware of the total context of that message. The total context in this sense means something like the exact message intended by the encoder. This study had been done with special reference to Egyptian social sciences undergraduates who had been asked to read social science texts written in English, though English was not their medium of instruction. It was found that most of them had difficulties. Some of the difficulties as observed were: they were more capable of extracting information from tables than passages as it required less linguistic skill, they more had difficulty in answering questions related to information implied in a passage than answering questions on details explicitly stated; they also faced problems in locating and forming comparison and contrast. They could not depict cause - effect relationships and they also faced problems in drawing conclusions from the given information in the passage. The main objective of this study was to point out the necessity of bringing across to students the organizational patterns of writing particularly relating to characteristics of their field of specialization. Special attention had been paid to Egyptian social science undergraduates, learning advanced reading in English. A technique for presenting the organizational pattern of a social science passage and a plan for directed reading activity revolving around had been suggested.

Carrell, P.L. (1983) [8] is Professor of Linguistic and ESL/EFL at Southern Illinois University at Carbondale. Her research interests, include the role of background knowledge and the interaction of text and reader in text comprehension. This study raised two issues, which are unresolved and found in both first language and second language research. These issues are:

a. The extent to which the previous research had either maintained or had confound the theoretical distinction between content and formal schemata, and the general nature of the relationship and interaction of these two types of schemata in a naturally occurring texts

b. The extent to which the effects measured by the cross-cultural research were related to more general situations of the presence or absence of appropriate background knowledge which may not be culture specific.

Research on psychological processes involved in reading-comprehension showed what a reader understands is a function of our past experiences and of our background knowledge. According to schema theory, the process of interpretation was guided by the principle that every input is mapped against existing schema and that all aspects of that schema must be compatible with the input information.

Langer, Judith A. (1986) [9] had done two experiments on writing to study and learn. The two studies examined the effects of writing on subject learning. For the first study, 322 ninth and eleventh grade students read passages from high school social studies and science textbook and engaged in six writing-to-study conditions. Students who wrote essays scored lower on immediate topic knowledge, while the students who used study methods other than essay writing had the greatest gains. The second study focused on the relationship between what writers do during different writing tasks and recall.110 students, who were ninth and eleventh graders, were the respondents. The students read two passages from the first study and engaged in four writing-to-study tasks. Findings indicated that the writing conditions led to greater recall of content than the non-writing condition. It was also shown that the more the content was manipulated during writing, the better it was recalled. Together, both studies indicated that the tasks such as questioning/answering and note-taking involved a superficial manipulation of the content. And it was this manipulation which led to extensive but short-lived learning.

Yael Bejarano (1987) [10] assessed the effects of two small groups of cooperative techniques (discussion group; student teams and achievement divisions) and the whole class methods on Academic achievement in EFL for 665 pupils in 33 seventh grade classes. Evaluation of pupils' achievement was conducted by observation and by special achievement tests administered before and after the experiment test. The finding revealed that group methods indicated greater improvement than the whole- class method on the total score of the test on the listening comprehension scale. The study demonstrated how to link the content to the process of instruction. Based on theoretical principles underlying this research and the findings, a cooperative small-group methodology in the language classroom was recommended. Implementation of this approach required intensive teacher training for use of the techniques, in terms of operational procedures in the classroom and in terms of appropriate design of the learning tasks.

James P. Lantolf (1994) [11] studied various aspects of second language learning informed by the socio-cultural theory of mind which was developed by the Russian psychologist Lev S. Vygotsky. The fundamental theoretical insight from Vygotsky's research was that higher forms of human mental activity are always, and everywhere, mediated by the symbolic means.

Mediation, whether physical or symbolic, was understood to be an introduction of an auxiliary device into an activity that links humans to the world of objects and to the world of mental behaviors. He reasoned that symbolic tools empower humans to organize and control such processes as attentiveness, logical problem-solving, planning, evaluation, memorization and intentional learning. Among symbolic tools are mnemonic devices, algebraic symbols diagrams, graphs, and language. According to Vygotsky, mental development arises as a consequence of the interaction of two distinct processes, one with biological roots and the other with socio-cultural origins. Through research it is demonstrated that once children begin to integrate symbols as auxiliary means of mediation into their physical and mental activity, this activity takes on a difficult and culturally influenced character.

Khaini Izwan Abdullah (1994) [12], as taken from Tickoo, M. L. (1994), reviewed about the current thinking in reading in order to draw some insights to form the basis of reading pedagogy. The study offered four guiding principles drawn from current views of reading pedagogy for language reading teachers. In brief those are

a) Component skills involved in reading should be practiced simultaneously.

b) The teacher as a facilitator facilitates the acquisition of reading skills by creating the suitable and necessary conditions for reading in the class which allows students to learn to read in a better way.

c) A thematic approach should be preferred for the selection of the texts. In a thematic approach students read a series of texts of a related topic. Such an approach allows the content, rhetorical structures and language to be built up.

d) The reading program should encourage extensive reading as repeated and extensive reading helps to build up linguistic schema which facilitates cognition of vocabulary.

The experiment was done on the varieties of activities with the aim of establishing, expanding and recycling a schema to facilitate the acquisition of reading skills. It was also suggested that the activities were compatible with both reading and language learning theories.

Lewis Larking (1994) [13], as taken from Tickoo, M. L. (1994), studied the reading comprehension ability of primary 5 and 6 children in Maley and English languages. The study was purposed for the evaluation of the relative strengths of a sample of Bruneian children at the primary level in reading comprehension in Malay and English languages. The study was also done to draw insight as to whether English was likely to threaten the position of reading in the Malay languages. The Edward's Reading Test was chosen to measure the reading comprehension ability of children in terms of grade levels. The test was comprised with a series of paragraphs which increased level of difficulty. Each paragraph was followed by a series of questions. Each student had to score at least seventy percent at a particular grade level. The result of the Malay reading test was in contrast to the English results. The result showed that forty three percent of children were able to read at above grade levels, whereas only thirty percent of the primary children achieved below grade level, for English. In Malay seventy -five percent of the children were reading at above grade level, while less than ten percent were below grade level, though a similar pattern of measurement was used. The study was about the reading comprehension ability of primary five and six children in Malay and English Languages in Brunei Darussalam. The purpose was to assess the relative strength of the children's comprehension ability in reading of English and Malay. It was indicated through the result that a great majority of children had an excellent ability at comprehending reading material in the Malay language. Further, it also indicated that the Malay language was not at all likely to be threatened by English.

In other study, Swati Vanniarajan (1994) [14], as taken from Tickoo, M. L. (1994), attempted to summarize the reading process in human information processing perspective, and their implications for future research in reading, in English, in Singapore. It was suggested that reading is an interactive process and it is a skill which develops along the continuum of controlled and automatic process. It was assumed that reading was an interactive process which involved a combination of information from two sources.

a) Linguistic information, i.e. the linguistic output received by the senses.
b) The related information already stored in memory i.e. the relevant linguistic and content knowledge derived from past experience.

The analysis of linguistic input coming from the reading material was called bottom-up processing. The influence of linguistic and content schemata in the interpretation of data was called top-down processing. It was assumed that second language reading, like first language reading, is also an interactive processing that requires the automaticity of decoding process for simultaneous executions of both top down and bottom up processing. It was also suggested that second language reading processes are time consuming, capacity demanding, sequential, and form oriented. The survey was done among 60 university students. It was reported that children did receive little or no encouragement from their parents for reading non-academic materials. They had very little or no time for reading while they were at school and also that academic and non-academic reading were synonymous. It was concluded that there might not be significant differences between native speakers of English and school educated speakers of English in Singapore, in their bottom up processing due to their acquisition of the skill since and through childhood. Bottom up processing might be automatic, cognitively undemanding and unconscious. Some qualitative differences were also shown between the two population in top down processing, which was likely to be due to the restricted and narrow reading in Academic English, less non-academic reading in both English and home language during primary, secondary and tertiary school years, neglect of reading in home language, diminishing use of home language, and decreasing role of ethic languages in the country.

Other collaborative work was on the nature of 'Engaged Reading' in classroom discussion of literature by Janice F. Almasi, Margaret G. Mckeown, and Isabel L. Beck (1996) [15], as taken from Dalton, B. (2001). They found that engaged reading occurred when students and teachers used interpretive tools to select, connect and organize information in the text to construct meaningful interpretations. In such engagement the three components observed are cognitive, metacognitive and motivational.

In their study Barbara Moss, Susan Leone and Mary Lou Dipillo (1997) [16] as cited from Bridget Dalton's Twenty Online Resources on reading with Comprehension and Engagement found how a teacher could improve through reading and writing of information trade books. They examined and described three ways in which children could be involved in such test

a. Reading and writing about information trade books.
b. Reading and writing settings of information trade books.
c. Reading and creating innovations on information trade books.

Aek Phakit (2006) [17] discussed the theoretical and pedagogical recall issues in second language reading comprehension and instruction. The aim was to provide an overview of second language strategic reading in the context of English as a second or a foreign language. Second language reading comprehension was viewed as highly complex, dynamic, multi-componential and multi-dimensional. It involved multiple interactions among reader factors (e.g. L_1 literacy, L_1 background, language proficiency, background knowledge, knowledge of genre and pragmatics, meta linguistic, knowledge, motivation, meta cognition and strategy use) and contextual factors (e.g. text topic and content, text type and genre, text readability, verbal and nonverbal communication). It was assumed that second language readers undergo the same reading behavior as they do in first language. Second language reading could be slower and less successful than first language reading. The only differences are the difference in first language and second language readers' vocabulary knowledge, types of response to difficult authentic text resources, awareness of language reading rates and fluency, cultural knowledge, role of the second language beginning for reading. Metacognition or strategic competence, which influences strategic reading, is an essential component of second language reading comprehension. It was discussed here that the roles of metacognition or strategic competence was a regulatory mechanism influencing strategic reading. Reading competence was related to human information processing framework. Metacognition or strategic competence which influences strategic reading was an essential component of second reading comprehension. The necessity was the understanding theoretical construct to make ESL/ EFL reading effective (particularly low ability learners and poor readers are in greater need of strategic reading instructions than good readers). This study also offers three models of strategic reading instruction.

Chaudron (2008) [18] surveyed the models and methods used for discovering the learners' processing of input. He has researched on second language learners' as input and the learners' intake. It was concluded that theories and models devised earlier used to develop consistent and well-developed models and methods for investigating language learner's processing of input. The theory and methodology of exploring the gap between target language input and its intake by second, learners is still in its early stages of development. Three important guidelines had been found: first we must exert more control over the independent variables under investigation; the next was that in order to achieve greater comparability across studies we must develop more standardized measure which would contrast the degree and the type of processing required by the learner; and third, we must attempt more systematically to develop and apply a model of intake processing that can be used to predict the results of our studies.

As Craigie (2008) [19] said in a study that teachers across disciplines and grade levels had discovered that writing essays and research papers can serve many purposes in the classroom. Theorists suggested that writing-across-the-curriculum is a variety of write-to-learn activities, from free writing in journals to summarizing class lectures to working with papers through multiple drafts. In the composition literature, supported for these activities had come largely from intuitive arguments about the value of writing as a way to learn. It was argued that one way in which writing helps to learn, is by forcing the learners to engage actively with the materials. It was also suggested that this active participation embedded the material more deeply in the memory. Writing was described as a cognitive activity. The arguments were that the process of writing forced learners to discover and articulate relationships between discrete fragments of knowledge and encouraged them to go beyond the text, to engage in imaginative and speculative thinking. It was also said in the study that writing could enhance students' learning in important and exciting ways, but the value of writing as a means for learning varies from one writing task to another, from one classroom to another, and from one student to the next. The research suggested four key variables in the relationship between writing and learning: the type of learning desired, the nature of the material to be learned, the nature of the writing task, and characteristics of writers themselves. Studies of writing-to-learn had defined learning in a number of ways. The easiest type of learning is through testing simple comprehension, particularly factual recall, and most experimental studies had included measures of this sort. Results on such type of learning had been mixed. When compared with non-writing activities such as answering, multiple-choice questions, writing appeared to help students remember and use facts from their reading. The research had demonstrated no clear advantage for extended or custom essay writing over shorter, more text-based writing activities when it came to factual recall or application measures. Finally, it was suggested in the study that the benefits of writing as an aid to basic comprehension might disappear as students became mature, indicating that younger students benefitted from the extra concentration and time-on-task that writing activities require. As students became more familiar with academic studies they develop efficient study strategies of their own.

As Singh (2008) [20] had found second language reading practice can involve a vast variety of materials.

a. Comic strips, advertisements, letters, articles, stories, newspapers, magazines, books, jigsaw reading exercise and so on.
b. Some theorists believe that through reading practice students will absorb and retain vocabulary by merely reading words in context without any special training in either vocabulary learning or reading.

It is justified by Krashen's recommendation, that students do "massive amounts of reading for pleasure," which he suggests will automatically increase their vocabulary. Krashen admitted that it is possible to make small gains in vocabulary learning effort, but this is not of equal value to that, because the time involved, and the better results could come through with massive reading alone.

2.1.3 The Value of Reading

Reading serves a unique purpose. It is like many things to many people. It is telescope through which one can look at the distant stars and speculates about life there. It is a microscope through which one cannot only examine the chromosomes and the atoms, but infer those minute particles which even the finest lenses cannot reveal. It is the only time-machine that can recreate the events of the past and open up the vistas of the future primitive men.

Reading is the means by which every age is linked to the other. It makes possible man's capacity for "time binding"-- the ability to perceive himself in the historic process and the fluid universe around him. It is an indispensable factor in modern life interwoven with work, recreation and other activities of young people and adults. Its great value lies in printed materials, which provides the most illuminating and varied records of human experience that are now available , and they can be examined and restudied again at the readers' convenience in acquiring clear understandings and in reading sound conclusions (DeBoer and Dallman,1960, pp: 3-12) [21].

2.1.4 Reading Purpose

There are many ways to read a text. It depends on our needs. These different ways can be reading intently, reading to make notes, glancing over someone else's shoulder, trying to guess the subject matter or so many purposes. Reading does not involve following a text with deep concentration to get a full appreciation of its meaning. Sometimes a text is scanned for a specific piece of information (e.g. finding telephone number in a phone book). At other times the content of a text is skimmed to gain a gist of the meaning (e.g. looking through a newspaper). Often, a text is closely read when detailed understanding is required (for example reading a novel). Such different ways of reading are not independent of each other. Often one type of reading leads to another. Skimming the catalogue may lead to close reading of a specific book/novel/magazine. Thus, in today's life reading is often motivated by a need or desire for information, required in order to complete an action e.g., a timetable is examined before a journey is made, a brochure is considered before a holiday is booked (Burnett and Myers,2004:42-43) [22].

Wallace (1998) [23] Described Three Kinds of Purposes of Reading

a) Reading for survivals : for example 'STOP' sign for motorist, 'danger' as a sign of prohibition to enter a dangerous zone; 'Enter' or 'Exit' signs: and others. Such kinds of reading are literally a matter of life and death.

b) Reading for learning: Reading is a means of finding out information. It serves the role of extending our general knowledge of the world.

c) Reading for pleasure: Here, reading is done for its own sake- we do not have to do it. If the readers do not read for pleasure in their mother tongue, they are very unlikely to do so in the second language also. Fluent readers are always motivated to read anything.

2.1.5 What Being a Good Reader Means?

Reading is part of our daily life. In a literate community we have different levels of readers: poor readers, good readers, beginners, adult readers. The purpose of reading is linked to different ways perceived for reading behavior, which are linked to situational context and also to social expectations – what kinds of language behavior is expected in classrooms, families, or particular religious settings. Our day to day reading behavior is highly selective. Earlier, reading was thought to consist of the skill of recognizing symbols and rendering their appropriate sounds. Sir John Adams described it as, 'Barking at Print'. Now, it is understood that reading is as much concerned with comprehension as it is with word recognition. The purpose is 'meaning making'. It requires a critical evaluation of ideas and thoughts. During the process of reading one does not only extract and comprehend the thoughts in the text being read, but one also reflects upon the thoughts extracted from the text read. A reader critically evaluates them and rejects, accepts, qualifies or judges the texts. This critical evaluation or reflection is as much a part of good reading as word recognition and comprehension (Fieldhouse (1957):14-15) [24].

Becoming an effective and fluent reader in another language has a number of important benefits for the learners like

- Reading in TL helps to consolidate that learning has taken place.
- It may help to increase the knowledge of the TL through exposure to new vocabulary and grammatical structures.
- Reading in TL is a new way of learning about the target culture.

- Becoming a fluent reader in TL is to acquire a life-long skill that helps the students maintain a competence and fluency in the TL, that may well outlast competence and fluency in speaking, listening and writing (Richard, R. Day (1993) p. no. ix) [25].

2.2 Reading Skills Involved in the Comprehension area

Reading is a meaning making process. Learning to recognize and remember the written word is only the first step. Once the words are identified, there remains the large and often difficult task of understanding what the words say. Comprehension appears to involve two stages:

1. The first stage occurs during the actual reading activity where the reader examines the message and simultaneously recognizes words and meaning through the graph emic, syntactic and semantic system.
2. The second stage can occur at any time, during and following the first stage. This stage is of comprehension and it might be best described as a reflective activity. The written message has been translated or received and can be subjected to more thoughtful analysis.

Theoretically, there must be an infinite number of mental operations that a reader makes in order to comprehend reflectively. Through factor analysis it has been found that a limited number of skills are used for varying purposes. A very small number of operational skills are used to understand an infinite variety of written messages.

The operational skills can be classified into three subgroups. Each group defines a comprehension purpose or process. These are

a) Comprehension as an informational process.

b) Comprehension as a thinking /manipulative process.

c) Comprehension as an evaluative /judgmental process.

Each of the three subgroups contains operational skills that are used to understand written messages. They include

A. Informational Processes

- Word meaning skills.
- Signalers of relationships
- Skills of contextual prediction.
- Recognition and memory for factual content

B. Manipulative Processes

- Classification and main idea thinking
- Inferential thinking

C. Evaluative Processes

- Judging the validity of the content
- Judging the author's purpose

Comprehension as an informational process suggests that the readers are trying to learn something from reading comprehension as a manipulative process. Readers can be expected to think about this information and they can explore its deeper implications and inferences. Comprehension as an evaluate process suggests that a message can be understood at both its information and manipulative levels and it can be acted upon [Duffy and Sharman (1977) pp.32-33] [26].

2.3 Reading Comprehension

Reading comprehension is the process of constructing meaning from the text. The goal of all reading instruction is ultimately targeted at helping a reader comprehend a text. Reading comprehension involves at least two people: the reader and the writer. The process of comprehending involves decoding the writer's words and then using background knowledge to construct an approximate understanding of the writer's message [27].

Reading comprehension skills separates the "passive" unskilled reader from the "active" readers. Skilled readers do not just read, they interact with the text. Reading comprehension skills increase the pleasure and effectiveness of reading. Strong reading comprehension skills help in all the other subjects and in the personal and professional lives [28].

We define reading comprehension as the process of simultaneously extracting and constructing meaning through interaction and involvement with written language. We use the words extracting and constructing to emphasize both the importance and the insufficiency of the text as a determinant of reading comprehension. Comprehension entails three elements

- The reader who is comprehending
- The text that is to be comprehended
- The activity in which comprehension is a part.

In considering the reader we include all the capacities, abilities, knowledge, and experiences that a person brings to the act of reading [29].

Reading is an act of communication. There is always a situation where a message is decoded by the reader. The goal is to receive a message correctly as it is intended by the writer. Thus, we have two goals of reading

- Word recognition (making the message read)
- Comprehension (Understanding)

The Goals of Reading Require Emphasis on Three Coding System

A. Graph emic
B. Syntactic
C. Semantic.

All these are Interrelated and Interconnected

A. **The Graph emic Symbols:** - The first sets of signals come from the printed letters and words. In a system, letters represent speech sounds and a child reads by associating these sounds with their visual representatives. The child learns how to look and what to look for and makes an association between what he or she sees. When these skills are learned, the child becomes an identifier of words.

B. **The Syntactic Signals:** - The second set of signals comes from the syntactic or grammatical structures of English language. When words are grouped into phrases, clauses, sentences or paragraphs, they are automatically arranged in accordance with the constraints of English grammar. As child translates the words from the page, she/he processes them into syntactical units and predicts the message. Accurate word recognition and the grammatical convention produce a continuous loop of meaning. The good reader guesses his/her way through the message using spelling and syntactic codes, each of which helps to make the other prediction more precise.

C. **Semantic Signals**: - Words which are grouped in phrases, sentences or paragraphs share not only the grammatical structure but also the common content. Each contributes to the message and as the child reads, he/she actively predicts what the meaning is. Constant feedback from the graph emic and syntactic systems allows children to verify or reject these predictions. The basic context of the message gives this insight. The more the child understands of the content of the message; the better will be this prediction of the future word identification and grammatical structures. Thus, the total process contains elements of both word recognition and comprehension [Duffy and Sherman (1977) pp: 13-15] [30].

2.4 Reading Processes

We assume that reading is a complex process, comprising many interrelated factors: language, visual discrimination, auditory discrimination, memory and cognitive development. An essential element inherent in this process is comprehension. Without this the process is incomplete. Much have been written and published on this topic, but no conclusive determinations have been reached [Sharma, (2006) p. no.215] [31].

A passage can properly be read with varying degrees of understanding. The scale of comprehension ranges from no meaning to complete understanding. The degree of desired comprehension will depend in part upon the purpose of the reader. There are variations in the degrees of comprehension, which exists within the individuals. The efficient reader is one who can adjust the degree of his comprehension to his objectives. There are some other factors which have a bearing upon comprehension and the physical condition of the reader, his interest in the material, and the difficulty of the selection—all of which affect understanding [Deboer and Dallman, (1960) p. no. 117] [32].

In the Wisconsin Design for Reading Skill Development (one of the skills management systems) comprehension skills have been clustered. It has identified six comprehension skills:

a) Main idea;

b) Sequence;

c) Reading for details;

d) Affixes;

e) Use of context; and

f) Reasoning.

(Sharma, P.L. (2006) pp. 218-219) [33]

Reading becomes a firmly established habitual activity, which an adult reader performs with great ease and speed. He is unaware of the various processes which he himself must carry out in reading. As a matter of fact a child cannot read unless he has developed an adequate knowledge of the words and of their meanings. For a normal child this comes through hearing and understanding of what is said to him and also through speaking words himself. He also manipulates and experiments with the production of speech sounds in his own language. The development of the facility in language increases familiarity not only with the sounds of words, but also with their meanings [Vernon, (1950) pp: I-36] [34].

Understanding a text is a constructive process that results in a coherent and integrated representation of the state of affairs described: a representation that is often referred to as a Mental Model or a Situational Model. To construct such a representation, the reader needs to engage in a number of processes. The reader needs to drive and integrate the meanings of the individual words, sentences, and paragraphs. Thus, there are many different reading skills which contribute to text comprehension. Three skills specifically associated with the construction of meaning are —

A. Inference making

B. Metacognition

C. Understanding Text Structures

One common factor in relation to the development of these reading-related skills is working memory capacity. Working memory refers to the system used to store and manipulate information simultaneously. It increases with age, together with gains in text comprehension [J Oakhill, and K Cain, (2006) p. no.382] [35].

2.4.1 Inference Making

This involves going beyond the literal content of the text through the generation of inferences. Inference can be used for the generation of inferences. Inference can be used to established referential coherence, causal antecedents to events, and characters' emotional reactions. Inferences can be distinguished into two main types: coherence and elaborative. Coherence references require that information explicitly provided in the text be integrated and/or that information be incorporated with information in the text itself to establish global coherence between different events, actions, and states in a text. Elaborative inferences beautify information in the text, but they are not strictly necessary to understanding. In effective and efficient comprehension, the emerging mental model of the text will be used to indicate where such gaps in comprehension occur and act as a signal to the reader that an inference is needed. Developmental studies show that young children are able to make the same inferences as older ones and they are also sensitive to the necessity of the inference. However, younger children do not make as many relevant inferences as older ones. There are several factors which limit their ability to generate inferences, e.g. knowledge of the world, prior knowledge, and knowledge about how to make inferences [J Oakhill, and K Cain, (2006) p. no.382] [36].

2.4.2 Metacognition

Metacognition about reading concerns knowledge about the purpose, goals, and processes of reading and the regulation of reading. Westby had given an overview of different types of metacognitive skills and their relation to reading ability:

Knowledge about reading: - Young children when interviewed, demonstrated a lack of awareness that they need to make sense of the text are more likely to report that reading is about 'getting the words right.' Beginner readers place a greater emphasis on word-reading accuracy than comprehension. It is because for them word-reading accuracy is likely to be the more salient and/or emphasized feature of reading.

Comprehension monitoring: - Here the concern is on the understanding of connected prose. Younger children are often unable to detect that crucial information is missing from a text and do not seem to realize when a text does not make sense. However, they are able to detect some errors. For example, young children are better at detecting lexical inconsistencies—made-up words—than internal inconsistencies, where two pieces of information on the text contradict each other.

Self-regulating of reading: - A skilled reader needs knowledge about reading strategies: how to read for different goals and purposes. In contrast to young children, older readers appreciate that someone might read a story more differently if their goal is to remember the story word for word than if the goal is to remember its meaning [J Oakhill, and K Cain, (2006) p. no.383] [37].

2.4.3 Understanding Text Structure

To understand how the ideas in a text are related to produce an interpretation of the text related to produce an interpretation of the text as a whole. Explicit awareness about the text structure, by certain common features of text may be useful aids for readers. It helps them to evoke relevant background information and schemas to facilitate the integration of different ideas in a text. This integration will depend on many skills and abilities, such as inference making, appreciating the main ideas in a text, and to understand how it is structured. The ability to identify the main idea in a text has been described as the essence of reading comprehension. Young readers have difficulties in recognizing the central theme or main ideas, and even sometimes find it hard to discriminate between relevant detail and irrelevant detail in a text. As children develop, they get better at selecting the main points in the text. They expect certain types of information to occur in texts and they can also add important details when retelling the texts [J Oakhill, and K Cain, (2006) p. no.383] [38].

2.5 Approaches To Reading

2.5.1 Top-Down Approach

Top-down reading models suggest that processing of a text begins in the mind of the readers with

- Meaning-driven processes, or
- An assumption about the meaning of a text.

From this perspective, readers identify letters and words only to confirm their assumptions about the meaning of the text. A top-down reading approach is a reading model that

- Emphasizes what the reader brings to the text;
- Suggests that reading is driven by meaning;
- Proceeds from whole part.

It is also known as inside-out model, concept driven model, whole to part model.

Here are Some Features of a Top-Down Approach to Reading

a) Readers can comprehend a selection even though they do not recognize each word.

b) Readers should use meaning and grammatical cues to identify unrecognized words.

c) Reading for meaning is the primary objective of reading rather than mastery of letters, letter/sound relationships, and words.

d) Reading requires the use of meaning activities rather than the mastery of a series of word-recognition skills.

e) The primary focus of instruction should be on reading the sentences, paragraphs, and whole selections.

The most important aspect about reading is the amount and kind of information gained from reading [39].

2.5.2 Bottom-Up Approach

A bottom-up reading model emphasizes a single-direction, part-to-whole processing of a text. In the beginning stages it gives little emphasis to the influences of the readers' world knowledge, contextual information and other higher-order processing strategies. Bottom-up approach is a reading model that:

- Emphasizes the written and printed text
- Suggests that reading is driven by a process that results in meaning (or, in other words, reading is driven by text)
- Proceeds from part to whole

Here are some features of bottom-up approach to reading. Bottom-up advocates believe the reader needs to

a) Identify letter features
b) Link these features to recognize letters
c) Combine letters to recognize spelling patterns
d) Link spelling patterns to recognize words and then proceed to sentence, paragraph and text level processing

The bottom-up approach requires that the meaning of any word must be decoded by the reader. It emphasizes the ability to decode what is seen in a text. However, it ignores emerging readers to recognize what they, as readers, bring to the information on the page. It is also known as part to whole model [40].

2.5.3 Interactive Approach

Both the bottom-up and top-down approaches are correct in the sense that a reader perceives, in bottom-up approach, the letters and words in a text and use his linguistic knowledge and the knowledge of the world, in top-down approach, to make meaning from the text. But the interpretation of a text is a matter of transaction, an act of communication, between the reader and the writer through the text (Zheng LIN (2002) pp.41) [41].

An interactive reading model is a reading model that recognizes the interaction of bottom-up and top-down processes, simultaneously, throughout the reading process. An interactive reading model attempts to combine the valid insights of bottom-up and top-down models. It attempts to take into account the strong points of the bottom-up and top-down models, and tries to avoid the criticisms leveled against each, making it one of the most promising approaches to the theory of reading today. It is a reading model that recognizes the interaction of bottom-up and top-down processes simultaneously, throughout the reading process. It emphasizes the role of prior knowledge or pre-existing knowledge in providing the reader with nonvisual or implicit information in the text. Both modes of information processing, top-down and bottom-up alike are seen as strategies that are flexibly used in the accomplishment of the reading tasks. Hence, the interactive approaches rely on both the graphic and contextual information [42].

According to Weaver (1998, p. 27) [43],

"............meaning is not in text itself, whether the text be literary or otherwise. Rather meaning arises during the transaction between reader and text. Thus reading is a process, a transaction between reader and text in a given situational context, and event during which meaning evolves."

The transactional nature of meaning making in reading indicates inconsistencies between writers' intention and readers' interpretation; and also in readers' interpretations of the same text. It seems impossible to find a single absolute meaning for a text, or to expect any interpretation identical to the writer's intention, because each individual's interpretation is unique (Zheng LIN (2002) pp.42-44) [44].

2.5.4 A Global Approach To Reading

A global approach to reading assumes that a person learns to read best when reading begins with natural and meaningful text. It is an approach that begins by giving learners natural, meaningful text to listen to, look at, and memorize by sight. Advocates of a global approach do not all agree on how to begin the task of teaching someone to read. Over the years advocates have identified their approach by their own label. Here are some of them: assisted reading, holistic reading, language experience approach, learning to read by reading, natural reading approach, neurological impress method, shared reading [Zheng LIN (2002)] [45].

In global approach the emphasis is given to the use of activities based upon specific reading and thinking skills, concepts, contents and issues of importance. The focus is on critical thinking and reading abilities such as formulating questions, identifying problems, gathering and categorizing information, making judgments, understanding different perspectives, recognizing bias and analyzing propaganda [46].

Thus a global approach to reading emphasizes to use designed activities as supplement by the teachers interested in helping students to improve their ability and to critically read the study materials with a global focus. In addition, teachers are provided with basic tools to use in assessing the readability materials [47].

Chapter - 3

Studies in Recall

3.0 Studies in Recall

It was as early as 1937 when Paul Thomas Young[1] conducted a study on the recall of pleasant and unpleasant words. The experiment was regarding cognition and memory. His primary aim in understanding it had been methodological. It was accepted that there is a valid distinction between the verbally stated meaning of pleasantness or unpleasantness. This experience of pleasantness or unpleasantness may or may not be reported. In this experiment two tests were employed simultaneously. One was a direct report of felt experience aroused by sensory stimulation, and the other was for the verbal expression of pleasant and unpleasant meanings. The students were asked to write down the words in list of column A and B as which they found pleasing or unpleasing words, respectively. The words might be nouns, verbs, adjectives, adverbs, or other parts of speech. The plan was made earlier, so it was possible to estimate the response. The notable thing which had been done is that there was no mention of the relative numbers of pleasant or unpleasant words; and also the amount of time to be spent in writing those words. One aim of the research was to study the ability of students to form pleasing and displeasing associations.

Aldridge and Farrell (1977) [2] had studied long-term recency effects in free recall. The result showed that invocation of a short-term store is unnecessary to explain recency effects in free recall. The purpose of this study was to determine whether positive recency would be obtained in such situation. The lists for free recall were constructed using three nouns as each item. Before and after each item the candidates counted backward by seven for 20 seconds. Visual presentation and auditory presentation were used in two different conditions. It is believed that a recency effect obtained under these conditions, particularly with auditory presentation, could safely be attributed to long-term storage. In order to maintain a total number of words per list only seven positions were used in the experiment. The list was too short to allow a primacy effect to develop. The magnitude of their primacy effect increased with the length of the list.

Langer, Judith A. (1986) [3] had done two experiments on writing to study and learn. The two studies examined the effects of writing on subject learning. For the first study, 322 ninth and eleventh grade students read passages from high school social studies and science texts and engaged in six writing-to-study conditions. Students who wrote essays scored lower on immediate topic knowledge, while the students who used study methods other than essay writing had the greatest gains. The second study focused on the relationship between what writers do during different writing tasks and recall.110 students, who were ninth and eleventh graders, were the respondents. The students read two passages from the first study and engaged in four writing-to-study tasks. Findings indicated that the writing conditions led to greater recall of content than the non-writing condition. It was also shown that the more the content was manipulated during writing, the better it was recalled. Together, both studies indicated that the tasks such as questioning/answering and note-taking involved a superficial manipulation of the content. And it was this manipulation which leads to extensive but short-lived learning.

Bohlmeyer, Elaine Morton, and others (1987) [4] studied the effects of spontaneous and imposed study strategies on recall of prose. Twenty college students were the respondents, read the passage from John Steinbeck's 'Log from the Sea of Cortez.' The effect of their study strategies on their recall of the idea units in the passage was tested. The students had to recall immediately after reading the passage and after a one week delay. The experiment which had been done provided a comparison of the effectiveness of two imposed study patterns: a written strategy and a relational strategy, with students' spontaneous study strategies. A control group was told to read the material, but was not told to study it. Subjects in the written strategy group were trained to write an outline of the passage as they read, while the subjects in relational strategy group mentally related information in the passage with something they had already known. The spontaneous group was untrained. Results indicated that the spontaneous group remembered significantly more idea units than other group. The findings showed that perhaps the mnemonic processes of college students could not be changed by merely instructing them to adopt a strategy; the training of the groups might not with have provided much practice; and interference from the training passages might have occurred. Recall of three importance levels (1 being most important, 2 moderately important and 3 being least important) was also tested, and it was shown that level 2 idea units were less recalled. It was suggested that for such kind of prose memorability and importance level were separate characteristics.

Donald J. Richgels; *et al.* (1987) [5] studied about the awareness of expository text. The purpose was to study the awareness of expository text structure (collection, comparison/contrast, causation, and problem solution) and the recall of texts written in those structures among six graders. Pupil's recall of main idea versus details and their recall of normal passages versus scrambled passages showed sensitive differences in reader's awareness of text structures. Experiment showed that pupils were highly aware of comparison/contrast structure and less aware of causation structure. It was found in this study that structure-aware students were more likely to use a structural strategy while reading than unaware students. Structure- awareness helped them to understand and remember the text. These six graders showed greater competence with comparison/contrast structure.

Patricia L. Carrel (1987) [6] had done an experiment to investigate the effects of culture-specific content schemata and formal schemata on ESL reading comprehension. During the study, high intermediate ESL students read, recalled, and answered questions about each of the two texts—one had a culturally familiar content, the other culturally unfamiliar content. Within each group half of the students read the text in a familiar, well organized, rhetorical format. The other half of the students read the texts in an unfamiliar, altered rhetorical format. The results indicated that content schemata affected reading comprehension to a greater extent than formal schemata.

Mark Sadoski and Zeba Quast (1990) [7] studied the relations between the mental imagery evoked in readers, the effective responses evoked in readers and readers' personal impressions of the relative importance of each text segment to the text as a whole. They also examined how these aspects of responses affected readers' long term recall of text. The study was conducted on 54 female under-graduate students. Three articles were used with materials. Students were asked to rate each paragraph in terms of its imagery, its affect or its importance relative to the article as a whole. After sixteen days they were asked to recall the important part of the texts read. The rating result showed that imagery and importance were not correlated in any of the articles. Moderate to high correlation was found between imagery and affect in all three articles. A significant correlation was found in one of the text in between the importance and affect in one of the paragraphs. The results of recall showed that ratings are given for imagery, affect and paragraph length. Correlation between importance and recall was negative for all the three articles. The highest response rating was given to imagery. Importance had received the lowest ratings. It was noted in the study that personal involvement and interest in the people and events mediate free recall.

Joan Hammadou (1991) [8] studied the interrelationships among prior knowledge, inference, and language proficiency in FL reading. The result of some findings at that time was that comprehension does not just mean understanding of words, sentences or even texts but it involves building a model within the mind of the reader. In this study it was found that readers deformed the surprise endings of stories when they were asked to read them to make the ending fit of the growing model that they created. Children recalled complex texts better than simplified ones. The cohesive nature of a complex text facilitated the model building process within the learners. In one of the studies it was demonstrated that cultural familiarity had a greater impact on comprehension than the pre-teaching of vocabulary. Lack of cultural knowledge slowed down the comprehension of text.

McDaniel, and others (1991) [9] were involved in a study about text expectancy, study strategies and recall of prose. The purpose was to explore how the readers modulate their reading strategies in accordance with how they expected to be tested. After reading three practice texts, the students were administered a test. The test was in line with their expectancies. They were asked to attempt a free-recall of a fairy tale or an expository text after reading it. The students expecting an essay test performed more organizational processing of the text than did those expecting other test formats. Therefore, in the recall of the fairy tale, there was no increase in recall due to the essay expectancy. Analysis and recall data indicated that recognition test expectancies produced little change in reading strategy.

Appel and Lantolf (1994) [10] investigated how speaking functions to mediate the cognitive activity of L1 and advancedL2 speakers/readers of English as they set out to read and recall a narrative and an expository text. This study showed how they understood from a text and the process through which they came to comprehend a text. A distinction was also drawn, during the study, between speaking to recall and speaking to understand. Analysis showed that the performance of the students depended on the interaction of individual and task. The results showed that both L1 and L2 speakers used the same strategies in attempting to recall and understand written texts. Students faced fewer problems in recalling the narrative text than expository text. Mediating speaking allowed readers to add more information to memory. The task was an integral part of the learning process. Giving such task was a way of knowing students' understanding of the texts through speaking.

Barry and Lazarte (1995) [11] studied the effects of embedded clauses on recall for English-speaking high school students. The texts which were used were historical texts in Spanish. The purpose of this study was twofold:

a) To assess the effect of additive clauses containing non- essential information on historical texts.
b) To compare the effect of recall among two groups:
    i. Those with higher prior knowledge of content domain,
    ii. Those with low prior knowledge.

It is hypothesized that longer text elicit less recall of the message compared to shorter texts. The data indicated that neither lexicon nor topic interacted with clause effect to decrease recall. As suggested that it was linguistic sensitivity acquired in mother-tongue which might constrain second language processing. This study hypothesized that content-based instruction written in Spanish for English speakers might require carefully adapted texts attention to teaching strategies for processing linguistic cues inherent in complex texts at the same level as native Spanish speakers.

Chun and Plass (1997) [12] based their research on theories of second language reading comprehension and text comprehension with multimedia. The purpose was to know how people comprehended texts in the second language with the help of multimodal instructional materials. They discussed how second language reading research focus was increasing the cognitive processes involved in reading, that is, the interaction of lower-level, bottom-up processes such as vocabulary acquisition with higher-level, top-down processes such as activating prior knowledge. They combined this knowledge with the current research on learning with multimedia, focusing on how learners integrate verbal and visual information, particularly with respect to the individual differences among learners that moderate learning processes. The process of reading and comprehending in one's native language (L1) is very complex, due to the countless number of factors that interact with each other in a non-linear and non-sequential manner. The issues and their accompanying complexity are further multiplied when describing and understanding reading comprehension in a second or foreign language (L2). In facilitating L2 reading comprehension, the use of sound, pictures, and animated pictures or video in addition to text have played an important role in vocabulary acquisition and in overall text comprehension, and are unquestioned components of instructional materials for language learning. Multimedia environments allow for the addition of visual and auditory information to a text in order to improve comprehension.

Oren Lamn (1997) [13] had studied two cases of poor spellers, in terms of recognition and recall of words' root letters. The study reported the two cases of poor spellers in Hebrew whose spelling errors could not be attributed to earlier obstruction in reading acquisition. The first subject was an adolescent native speaker of Hebrew with normal IQ, a student in a regular class whose reading achievements in tests given to him on several occasions between the ages of 8 and 14 were average, but his spelling did not improve over the years. The second subject was a 24-year-old mentally retarded man whose vocal reading of unvowelled Hebrew texts was almost normal in spite of very poor understanding of text content. He marked extremely poor spelling, which contrasted with his vocal reading achievements. A reading and writing test was employed to test the hypothesis of dissociation between recognition and recall of words' orthography in these cases, but the hypotheses was not confirmed. Both subjects could read correctly different homophonic graphs that differed in one of their root letters but they were unable to properly assign each to its meaning as indicated by the difference in spelling. On the other hand, both subjects could efficiently use similar differences in spelling between words in a pair in cases where the orthographic difference indicated different pronunciations. It was suggested that the two-stage phonological model has several advantages in explaining development dissociations between skilled vocal reading and spelling ability.

Farzad Sharifian (2001) [14] study was about the Mnemonic influence of self-cues on narrative recall. It was an extension of research on the effect of self-versus other generated cues on memory.ESL learners were the informants. The purpose was to see if language status would have a bearing on effectiveness of memory process. TOEFL tests of proficiency was administered to a group of 50 male participants aged 23 to 28. The results were

a) Self-generated retrieval cues subsequent to recall and this had an important facilitating effect on the recall of narrative texts, when inspection of the generated lists during written recall was not allowed.

b) Self-generated retrieval cues subsequent to recall had an important facilitating effect on the recall of a narrative text when the inspection of the generated list during written recall was allowed.

c) There is no significant recall advantage for the inspection over the non-inspection.

Participants were tested Under Two Conditions

i. Advanced listing condition (students are not allowed to inspect their self-generated cues).

ii. Posterior listing condition (students are allowed to inspect their self-generated cues).

Shagufta Imtiaz (2004) [15] had done a research on the gender differences in recall in expository writing among children who are eighth graders. Three expository texts are given (comparison/contrast, problem/solution, and description). The task was to identify the main idea and to attempt a written recall. The response recalled texts were compared with the original texts. As a result of experiment, some differences in recall had been shown among both groups. In the recall of idea units of the topic sentence, boy's recall for comparison/contrast was highest. Then for descriptive and for problem solution, it was the lowest. Among girls the highest score was of the descriptive passage; then for problem/solution and then for comparison/contrast. The passages with a relatively smaller sentence as the last line had shown had a better recall. Students also used their own sentences to end the recalled passage.

Patricia L. Carrel (2006) [16] researched the awareness of text structure. Research with native speakers' of English has shown differences in speakers' awareness of particular expository text structures (comparison/contrast, description, causation, and problem solution) and their recall of texts written in those structures. This study was designed to investigate the relationships between EFL/ESL readings. Forty-five high-intermediate ESL students were the informants. They were asked to attempt a written recall task of both comparison/contrast and collection of description texts. Two different measures of awareness were:

a) Use of organization in written recall; and

b) Recognition of organization in response to a probe question.

Recall showed that there were no differences in levels of awareness, regardless of how it was measured, due to differences in text structures. There were differences in the quality of information recalled as a function of text structure. Those students who used the structure of the reading passages to organize written recalls showed superior recall both quantitatively and qualitatively in terms of relationships between awareness and recall.

Yuh-Fang Chang (2006) [17] studied the comparison of readers' performance on the immediate recall and a translation task, in order to explore the effect of memory on readers' recall. All participants were native speakers of Mandarin Chinese whose ages ranged from 20 to 22. The results showed that the translation task yielded significantly more evidence of comprehension than did the immediate recall task, which indicates that the requirement of memory in the recall task hinders test-takers' ability to demonstrate fully their comprehension of the reading passage. The results also showed that the significant difference found in learners' performance between the immediate recall and the translation task spanned the effect of topics and proficiency levels. It was assumed that the immediate written recall task was a widely used measure of both first language (L1) and second language (L2) reading comprehension, and had been advocated over traditional test methods such as multiple choice, cloze tests and open-ended questions because it is a direct and integrative assessment task. However, it had also been criticized as it requires memory. Whether and how the requirement of memory biased the understanding of readers' comprehension remained unexplored.

As Craigie (2008) [18] said in a study that teachers across disciplines and grade levels had discovered that writing essays and research papers can serve many purposes in the classroom. Theorists suggested that writing-across-the-curriculum is a variety of write-to-learn activities, from free writing in journals to summarizing class lectures to working with papers through multiple drafts. In the composition literature, support for these activities had come largely from intuitive arguments about the value of writing as a way to learn. It was argued that one way in which writing helps to learn, is by forcing the learners to engage actively with their material. It was also suggested that this activity embedded the material more "deeply" in memory. Writing was described as a "connective" activity, the arguments here were that, the process of writing forces learners to discover and articulate relationships between what might otherwise be discrete bits of knowledge and encouraged them to go beyond the text, to engage in imaginative and speculative thinking. It was also said in the study that writing could enhance students' learning in important and exciting ways, but the value of writing as a means for learning varies from one writing task to another, from one classroom to another, and from one student to the next. The research suggested four key variables in the relationship between writing and learning: the type of learning desired, the nature of the material to be learned, the nature of the writing task, and characteristics of writers themselves. Studies of writing-to-learn had defined learning in a number of ways. The easiest type of learning is through testing simple comprehension, particularly factual recall, and most experimental studies had included measures of this sort. Results on such type of learning had been mixed. When compared with non-writing activities such as answering, multiple-choice questions, writing appeared to help students remember and use facts from their reading. The research had demonstrated no clear advantage for extended or custom essay writing over shorter, more text-based writing activities when it came to factual recall or application measures. Finally, it was suggested in the study that the benefits of writing as an aid to basic comprehension might disappear as students became mature, indicating that younger students benefitted from the extra concentration and time-on-task that writing activities require. As students became more familiar with academic studies they develop efficient study strategies of their own.

Chapter - 4

Methodology and Analysis

4.0 Methodology and Analysis

4.1 Method

Participants. A survey was conducted with the early intermediate students of Language Arts, at Senior Secondary School, in Aligarh. Among the group there were 15 boys and 15 girls, aged 16-17 years, who were the informants. They were studying English as an optional subject with other social science subjects. Among boys most of them were Hindi (14) and Urdu (11) speakers, and in addition some of them had also been familiar with other languages also, such as, Arabic (1) Sanskrit (2), Bengali (2) and French (1). Among the group of girls most of them were Urdu (14) and Hindi (12) speakers. There was only one girl who was familiar with Malyalam, in addition to that. All the students were multilingual. And they were able to use English language fluently as a second language.

Materials. An expository passage (cause/effect) had been selected for the experiment. The untitled passage was unseen and related to the food habits in modern time. It was in accordance with the level of the learners. In addition, a sheet was given to the students with few questions relating to their background and exposure to the topic. The same passage was used with both the groups (see appendix-II).

Administration. A pre-reading exercise was conducted with both the groups of the learners. This was an imitation exercise used to acquaint the learners with the unseen passage. The pre-reading questions were related to the food habits in the modern world. The pre-reading activity conducted on the groups by using brain-storming and semantic mapping as a technique. The numbers of responses were recorded. The second step was to read the passage slowly. The respondents were told that they would be asked to recall the passage. The respondents were then asked to give a suitable title and to recall the passage which they had already heard. The time given was 30 minutes (see appendix II).

Assessment. The respondents of both the groups were assessed on the basis of the passage recalled. The assessment was based on two things: a) the total number of words, clauses, and sentences recalled; and b) how much close the recalled clauses are to the original clauses in the passage. This suggests that learners were rated on the basis of the closeness of the clausal units in the original text.

4.2 Analysis

Likert Scale

As a preliminary to the reading comprehension passage, a likert scale was distributed to the candidates. This was given after the respondents were told about the passage and the topic. The questions were divided into two sections (see Appendix I). Section-I of the questionnaire included close-ended responses of the students and section-II consisted of open-ended responses. The first section consisted of four questions (see the table no. 1). In question no. 1 and 3 four point scales were used, rating from 'a lot,' 'some,' 'a little bit,' and 'nothing'. In question no. 2 three point scales was used that is 'a lot' 'not much' and 'not at all'. Question no.4 used agreement likert scale, i.e. Yes/No. The values are not assigned to these questions. Analysis of the data included frequency, percent, valid percent, cumulative percent; standard deviation, Pearson's coefficient correlation and reliability through Cronbach's alpha (see tables- 9, 10, 11, 12, 13 and 16). Pearson product moment correlation was used to analyze the four items of clausal unit. To determine the reliability of the test Cronbach's alpha reliability (.633) was used. Lenene's test for equality of variance was used (see table-17).

Section - I

The rating of the section-I was as follows:

Table 1

Section one	Ratings	
Question 1	4 point scale	A lot Some A little bit Nothing
Question 2	3 point scale	A lot Not much Not at all
Question 3	4 point scale	A long essay A short essay A few sentences Nothing
Question 4	2 point scale	Yes No

Boys

The numbers of languages known among the boys were: English (15), Hindi (14), Urdu (11), Sanskrit (2), Bengali 2), Arabic (1) and French (1). Among 15 boys, the response to the first question was 60%, to their familiarity with the topic, while 33% boys knew a lot about the topic. Only one student stated that he knew a little bit about the topic. In the second question, which was about their interests to the topic, 80% stated that they were not much interested in the topic, and 20% respondents showed their interest about the topic. In the third question which was about whether they could write a paragraph on the topic, 60% stated that they could write a short essay 20% stated that they could write a few sentences and 20% marked that they could write a long essay. The last question was whether they could think of any work on the same topic, to which 67% replied positively while 33% gave a negative reply.

Girls

The numbers of languages known among the girls were: English (15), Hindi (14), Urdu (11), Sanskrit (2), Bengali (2), Arabic (1) and French (1). In the girls' category, the first question was their familiarity with the topic. Among the 15 respondents 60% stated that they were familiar with the topic while 40% stated that they knew a lot about the topic. The second question was whether the topic interests them. In response to this 67% stated that it interested them a lot. While 33% stated that it did not interest them much. In the third question which was about whether they could write a paragraph on the topic, 40% stated that they could write a short essay 34% stated that they could write a few sentences and 26% marked that they could write a long essay. The last question was whether they could think of any work on the same topic, to which 53% replied positively while 47% gave a negative reply.

Section - II

The rating of the section-II was as follows

The students were asked to give a suitable title to the passage listened by them. The untitled passage had been given so many titles by the respondents. The titles given by them showed their understanding of the passage, and it was found that their interpretation of the passage varied from each other's. Some of the selected titles are

From Male Group

a) Advancement in Technology in Food Cooking
b) Cooking Food in Modern Age
c) Changes in food Consumption in the 21st Century
d) Food of Modern world with New Technologies

e) Preparation of Food in Modern World

f) Modern Day Cooking

g) Fast Food Replacing Traditional One

h) Convenience in Food Preparation

i) Changing Interests and Aspects in the Modern World Age Regarding Food

From Female Group

a) Changing food Pattern among People

b) Modern World

c) Twentieth Century--- The Modern Food World

d) The changes Brought About the 20th Century

e) Technological Advancement

f) Advancement in Modern World

g) Technological Advancement in Food Making

h) Changing Style of Food

i) Changing Technology Makes Life Simpler

j) Technological Advancement in Food Preparation

Though, the titles are different, but are related to a single idea i.e. food making and eating. All the titles are showing the estimated interpretation of the respondents. The passage was selected according to the level of the students.

In terms of open-ended response, the assessment was done on the basis of the total number of words, clauses and sentences recalled (see table no.7 and 8). A comparison was made, in between, the original and what was recalled by both the groups, in terms of the passage written by the respondents, individually. The category of recalled clauses was also marked through pointer's scale (see table no. 1).

Table 2: Boys

No. of respondents	Exact clause	Very closely related	Not very closely related	Totally different
1	1(3%)	4(12%)	2(6%)	9(27%)
2	0	5(15%)	0	8(24%)
3	0	4(12%)	5(15%)	3(9%)
4	0	1(3%)	4(12%)	10(30%)
5	0	3(9%)	3(9%)	1(3%)

6	0	0	2(6%)	5(15%)
7	1(3%)	1(3%)	5(15%)	11(33%)
8	0	1(3%)	2(6%)	4 (12%)
9	1(3%)	6(18%)	3(9%)	2(6%)
10	0	0	1(3%)	7(21%)
11	1(3%)	1(3%)	4(12%)	0
12	0	0	4(12%)	10(30%)
13	0	2(6%)	3(9%)	6(18%)
14	6(18%)	1(3%)	6(18%)	7(21%)
15	1(3%)	7(21%)	1(3%)	3(9%)
Total: -	11	36	45	87

Table 3: Girls

No. of respondents	Exact clause	Very closely related	Not very closely related	Totally different
1	4(12%)	4(12%)	2(6%)	2(6%)
2	3(9%)	2(6%)	6(18%)	6(18%)
3	3(9%)	4(12%)	7(21%)	4(12%)
4	3(9%)	5(15%)	1(3%)	6(18%)
5	1(3%)	3(9%)	6(18%)	2(6%)
6	2(6%)	1(3%)	8(24%)	5(15%)
7	3(9%)	4(12%)	3(9%)	5(15%)
8	10(30%)	5(15%)	5(15%)	2(6%)
9	2(6%)	6(18%)	6(18%)	1(3%)
10	3(9%)	2(6%)	3(9%)	1(3%)
11	7(21%)	8(24%)	3(9%)	1(3%)
12	1(3%)	5(15%)	9(27%)	1(3%)
13	9(27%)	2(6%)	10(30%)	1(3%)
14	3(9%)	3(9%)	6(18%)	4(12%)
15	6(18%)	8(24%)	2(6%)	1(3%)
Total: -	60	62	77	42

Table 3: Girls

No. of respondents	Exact clause	Very closely related	Not very closely related	Totally different
15	60	62	77	42

Table 4: Boys

No. of respondents	Exact clause	Very closely related	Not very closely related	Totally different
15	11	36	45	87

Table 5: (Boys)

No. of Observant	(a)	(b)	(c)	(d)
1	i	ii	ii	i
2	ii	ii	ii	i
3	ii	ii	iii	ii
4	i	ii	iii	ii
5	iii	ii	ii	ii
6	ii	ii	ii	ii
7	Ii	ii	ii	ii
8	i	ii	ii	i
9	i	i	i	i
10	i	i	ii	i
11	ii	ii	iii	i
12	ii	ii	ii	i
13	ii	ii	ii	i
14	ii	i	i	i
15	ii	ii	i	i

Table 6: (Girls)

No. of Observant	(a)	(b)	(c)	(d)
1	ii	i	iii	i
2	i	i	i	i
3	Ii	i	i	i
4	i	I	i	i
5	ii	Ii	iii	ii
6	ii	I	iii	ii
7	ii	ii	ii	ii
8	i	ii	i	i
9	i	Ii	ii	ii
10	ii	Ii	iii	ii
11	ii	Ii	ii	ii
12	ii	I	iii	i
13	ii	I	ii	i
14	i	i	ii	i
15	i	i	ii	ii

Table 7: Boys

(1)

	Words	Clauses	Sentences
Original text	233	33	17
Text written	106 (45%)	16 (48%)	6 (35%)

(2)

	Words	Clauses	Sentences
Original text	233	33	17
Text written	116 (49%)	13 (39%)	7 (41%)

(3)

	Words	Clauses	Sentences
Original text	233	33	**17**
Text written	68 (29%)	12 (36%)	5 (29%)

(4)

	Words	Clauses	Sentences
Original text	233	33	17
Text written	106 (44%)	14 (42%)	6 (35%)

(5)

	Words	Clauses	Sentences
Original text	233	33	17
Text written	60 (25%)	7 (21%)	5 (29%)

(6)

	Words	Clauses	Sentences
Original text	233	33	17
Text written	55 (23%)	7 (21%)	6 (35%)

(7)

	Words	Clauses	Sentences
Original text	233	33	17
Text written	104 (44%)	18 (54%)	7 (41%)

(8)

	Words	Clauses	Sentences
Original text	233	33	17
Text written	55 (23%)	7 (54%)	4 (41%)

(9)

	Words	Clauses	Sentences
Original text	233	33	17
Text written	94 (40%)	12 (36%)	5 (29%)

(10)

	Words	Clauses	Sentences
Original text	233	33	17
Text written	59 (25%)	8 (24%)	5 (29%)

(11)

	Words	Clauses	Sentences
Original text	233	33	17
Text written	42 (18%)	6 (18%)	3 (17%)

(12)

	Words	Clauses	Sentences
Original text	233	33	17
Text written	82 (35%)	14 (42%)	5 (29%)

(13)

	Words	Clauses	Sentences
Original text	233	33	17
Text written	74 (31%)	11 (33%)	5 (29%)

(14)

	Words	Clauses	Sentences
Original text	233	33	17
Text written	126 (54%)	20 (60%)	10 (58%)

(15)

	Words	Clauses	Sentences
Original text	233	33	17
Text written	65 (27%)	12 (36%)	4 (23%)

Table 8: Girls

(1)

	Words	Clauses	Sentences
Original text	233	33	17
Text written	87 (37%)	12 (36%)	6 (35%)

(2)

	Words	Clauses	Sentences
Original text	233	33	17
Text written	95 (40%)	17 (51%)	6 (35%)

(3)

	Words	Clauses	Sentences
Original text	233	33	17
Text written	108 (46%)	17 (51%)	7 (41%)

(4)

	Words	Clauses	Sentences
Original text	233	33	17
Text written	113 (48%)	15 (45%)	8 (47%)

(5)

	Words	Clauses	Sentences
Original text	233	33	17
Text written	79 (33%)	11 (33%)	6 (35%)

(6)

	Words	Clauses	Sentences
Original text	233	33	17
Text written	84 (36%)	14 (42%)	5 (29%)

(7)

	Words	Clauses	Sentences
Original text	233	33	17
Text written	83 (35%)	14 (42%)	7 (41%)

(8)

	Words	Clauses	Sentences
Original text	233	33	17
Text written	165 (70%)	24 (72%)	9 (52%)

(9)

	Words	Clauses	Sentences
Original text	233	33	17
Text written	77(33%)	15(45%)	5(29%)

(10)

	Words	Clauses	Sentences
Original text	233	33	17
Text written	58 (24%)	9 (27%)	5 (29%)

(11)

	Words	Clauses	Sentences
Original text	233	33	17
Text written	131 (56%)	19 (57%)	9 (52%)

(12)

	Words	Clauses	Sentences
Original text	233	33	17
Text written	224 (96%)	15 (45%)	10(68%)

(13)

	Words	Clauses	Sentences
Original text	233	33	17
Text written	106 (45%)	22 (66%)	9 (52%)

(14)

	Words	Clauses	Sentences
Original text	233	33	17
Text written	76 (32%)	16 (48%)	5 (29%)

(15)

	Words	Clauses	Sentences
Original text	233	33	17
Text written	76 (32%)	17 (51%)	6 (35%)

Table 9: Frequency Table (BOYS)

Q1. How much do you know about this topic?

	Frequency	Percent	Valid Percent	Cumulative Percent
Valid 1.00	5	33.	33.	33.
2.00	9	60.0	60.0	93.
3.00	1	7.	7.	100.0
Total	15	100.0	100.0	

Q2. Does the topic interest you?

	Frequency	Percent	Valid Percent	Cumulative Percent
Valid 1.00	3	20.0	20.0	20.0
2.00	12	80.0	80.0	100.0
Total	15	100.0	100.0	

Q3. Can you write a paragraph on this topic?

	Frequency	Percent	Valid Percent	Cumulative Percent
Valid 1.00	3	20.0	20.0	20.0
2.00	9	60.0	60.0	80.0
3.00	3	20.0	20.0	100.0
Total	15	100.0	100.0	

Q4. Can you think of any other work on the same topic?

	Frequency	Percent	Valid Percent	Cumulative Percent
Valid 1.00	10	67.	67.	67.
2.00	5	313	33.	100.0
Total	15	100.0	100.0	

Table 10: Frequency Table (GIRLS)

Q1. How much do you know about this topic?

	Frequency	Percent	Valid Percent	Cumulative Percent
Valid 1.00	6	40.0	40.0	40.0
2.00	9	60.0	60.0	100.0
Total	15	100.0	100.0	

Q2. Does the topic interest you?

	Frequency	Percent	Valid Percent	Cumulative Percent
Valid 1 00	9	60J	60J	60J
200	6	40.0	40.0	100.0
Total	15	100.0	100.0	

Q3. Can you write a paragraph on this topic?

Frequency		Percent	Valid Percent	Cumulative Percent
Valid 1.00	4	27.	27.	27.
2.00	6	40.0	40.0	67.
3.00	5	33.	33.	100.0
Total	15	100.0	100.0	

Q4. Can you think of any other work on the same topic?

	Frequency	Percent	Valid Percent	Cumulative Percent
Valid 1.00	8	53.	53.	53.
2.00	7	47.	47.	100.0
Total	15	100.0	100.0	

Table 11: Mean and Standard Deviation

	N	Mean	Std. Deviation
q1	15	2.	1.
q2	15	1.8000	0.
q3	15	2.0000	1.
q4	15	1.	0.
Valid N (Iistwise)	15		

Table_12: Correlations

	Q1	Q2	Q3	Q4
Q1 Pearson Correlation	1	0.	.600*	0.
		1.	0.	0.
Q2 Pearson Correlation		1	0.	.600*
			1.	0.
Q3 Pearson Correlation			1	0.
				0.
Q4 Pearson Correlation				1

Table 13: Reliability

Cronbach's Alpha	N of items
.633	4

Table 14: Male

	N	Mean	Std. Deviation	Std. Error Mean
Exact clause	15	.7333	1.53375	.39601

	N	Mean	Std. Deviation	Std. Error Mean
Very closely related	15	2.4000	2.29285	.59210

	N	Mean	Std. Deviation	Std. Error Mean
Not very closely related	15	3.0000	1.69031	.43644

	N	Mean	Std. Deviation	Std. Error Mean
Totally different	15	5.7333	3.49421	.90220

Table 15: Female

	N	Mean	Std. Deviation	Std. Error Mean
Exact clause	15	4.0000	2.75162	.71047

	N	Mean	Std. Deviation	Std. Error Mean
Very closely related	15	4.1333	2.09989	.54219

	N	Mean	Std. Deviation	Std. Error Mean
Not very closely related	15	5.1333	2.72204	.70283

	N	Mean	Std. Deviation	Std. Error Mean
Totally different	15	5.7333	3.49421	.90220

Table 16: Mean and Standard Deviation

	N	Mean		Std.	Variance	Kurtosis	
	Statistic	Statistic	Std. Error	Deviation, Statistic	Statistic	Statistic	Std. Error
Exact clause	30	2.3667	.5017	2.74783	7.551	1.466	.833
Very closely related	30	3.2667	.4260	2.33317	5.444	-.678	.833
Not very closely related	30	4.0667	.4522	2.47656	6.133	-.118	.833
Totally different	30	4.2667	.5772	3.16155	9.995	-.666	.833
Valid N (listwise)	30						

Table 17: Levine's Test of Equality of Variance

T-test for equality of means

		Levene's Test for Equality of Variarces		T-Test for Equality of Means						
		F	Sig.	t	DF	Sig. (2-tailed)	Mean Difference	Std. Erro-Difference	95% Confidenc Interval of the Difference	
									Lower	Upper
Exact clause	Equal variances assumed	5.586	.025	4.016	28	.000	3.2667	.81338	1.60053	4.93280
	Equal variances not assumed			4.016	21.934	.001	3.2667	.81338	1.57952	4.95381
very closely related	Equal variances assumed	.554	.463	2.159	28	.040	1.7333	.80277	.08893	3.37774
	Equal variances not assumed			2.159	27.786	.040	1.7333	.80277	.08836	3.37831
not very closely related	Equal variances assumed	4.420	.045	2.579	28	.015	2.1333	.82731	.43866	3.82800
	Equal variances not assumed			2.579	23.399	.017	2.1333	.82731	.42352	3.84314
totally different	Equal variances assumed	6.177	.019	-2.832	28	.008	-2.9333	1.03586	-5.05521	-.81146
	Equal variances not assumed			-2.832	22.092	.010	-2.9333	1.03586	-5.08107	-.78566

Conclusion

Results and Discussion

Girls

The highest among the 'exact clause' category was 30% followed by 27%, 18% and 12% with the lowest being 3% (Among the 'very closely related' category the highest is 24% followed by 18%, 13% and the lowest 8%. In the category of 'not very closely related' the highest was 30%, 27%, 24% with the lowest being 3%. In the 'totally different' category the highest is 18% any 2, followed by 18% any 2 and 25% any 2. Among the reform categories the highest number of sentences formed is in the third category what is 'not very closely related'. This indicates the ability of the learners to recall the sentences and to reproduce it with changes in the sentence structure, but not at the level of meaning. The total number of 'very closely related' sentences is 62 followed by 'exact clause' which is 60. This demonstrates the significant differences in the recall of idea units among the learners. The learners had been briefed about the pre-writing plan where recall was related to listening. It is possible that if they had read the passage, been given more time, the recall would have improved. The last category of 'totally different' clauses is also significantly a large number, which suggests the comprehension failure on the part of the learners. It could also be attributed to the lack of background knowledge among learners.

Boys

Among the boys the highest 'exact clauses' category was 18% in case of only one student with a dismal level among the others. Most of the boys did not have 'exact clause'. In their recall in 'very closely related' category the highest was 21% followed by 18% and 15%. In the next category the highest was 18% followed by 15% among 2 boys and 12% among 2 others boys. The result was more evident in the 'totally different' category with the highest at 33%. In the total number of sentences among the various categories, the highest was in the 'totally different' category followed by 'not very closely related' and the smallest no was in the 'exact clause'.

This highest number was seen in the 'totally different' clauses recalled, for which a number of reasons could be attributed, one of which could be the lack of passage comprehensibility. Another reason could be the background knowledge of the subjects. The number of exact clauses among boys is seen only in one student, and it is in the 'totally different' category that the highest number is traced. It also depicts the attempts of the learners to write the passage in their own words while retaining the meaning of the passage. The original passage has 233 words and the highest number of words used by boys is 136, while the lowest is 6. The maximum number of learners falls in the range of 151 words, which suggests the reductions in the recalled passage and the different ways in which that is summarized. Similar trend is involved in case of clauses and sentences.

Comparison

Among the girls the highest number is 113 words out of a total of 233. The average number of words used ranges between 75– 110 which is higher than that of boys. Among the 15 respondents 10 have used words above 75 in number. Similarly, in case of clauses the number of clauses among girls is higher. In case of girl, the total number of clauses in the original is 33, and 14 respondents have used more than 10 clauses (see table no. 8 and 9). The number of words, clauses and sentences used by girls depicts the comprehensibility and recall among the respondents. The recalled passage shows summarization while the respondents are depicted in the reduced number of words and clauses used. The response of the girls as being better than that of the boys could also be attributed to the passage familiarity. The passage deals with food preparation in Modern time which is a familiar topic for girls.

A comparison of the statistics of boys and girls shows the significant differences among the recalled passages of the both groups. (see table no. 15 and 16). Among the boys the recalled passage shows the maximum number of difference and minimum number of exact clauses. In case of girls the maximum number is in the 'not very closely related' category and the minimum is in 'totally different' category. The use of the 'exact clause' in the recalled passage may suggest retention and retrieval of the passage which had been listened to by the learners (see table no. 4 and 5). A better result as far as recall is concerned, could have been obtained if the passage had been given to the learners to read for a second time. Despite the better performance of the girls much still needs to be improved in the recalled items. The highest number of recalled items among the girls is still low and needs to be improved. These are pointers towards memory selective attention and comprehension.

Another significant point, responsible for such a variation in the responses from both the groups, might be their interest about the topic, as it had been seen in the first section of the questionnaire. In the second question, which was about their interest in the topic, girls stated that they knew a lot about the topic, while boys were not much interested in that. Thus, the topic did not match the interest of the boys, and hence, the total number of exact clauses recalled by the boys, that is 11, was much less than that of the total number of exact clauses recalled by the girls, that is, 60 (see table no. 6 and 7).

Another noticeable thing, which had been found among both the groups, was the variation in 'claimed control and actual performance'. If the students' performance for the responses in the section-I was compared with section-II, in terms of exact clauses recalled, then, this variation could be easily defined. Among the group of girl respondents (2, 4, 9, 14, and 15), they stated their likelihood about the topic as they marked in first option, in the second question, that was 'a lot.' But, later, what they had actually recalled in the category of exact clauses was 51%, 45%, 48%, 48%, and 51% respectively. Among the group of boys the respondents (1, 4, 8, 9, and 10), what they recalled in the category of exact clauses was (48%, 42%, 21%, 36%, and 24%) respectively (see table no. 2-3 and 5-6).

Appendices

Appendix I

Section - 1

1. Name: ____.

2. Age: ____.

Languages known: ______________________________.

________________________________.

________________________________.

________________________________.

________________________________.

3. Male/Female: ________________________________.

4. Tick mark the option which is preferable to you, in the following questions.

a) How much do you know about this topic?

i. A lot ☐

ii. Some ☐

iii. A little bit ☐

iv. Nothing ☐

b) Does the topic impress you/ how much the topic convinced you?

i. A lot ☐

ii. Not much ☐

iii. Not at all ☐

c) Can you write a paragraph on this topic?

i. A long essay ☐

ii. A short essay ☐

iii. A few sentences ☐

iv. Nothing ☐

d) Can you think of any other work on the same topic?

i. Yes ☐

ii. No ☐

Section - 2

Title: ______________________________

Appendix II

I. Pre-reading

a) How has the eating habit been offered in the modern world?

b) What do you think about fast food?

c) What are the advantages and disadvantages of fast food?

d) What are the advantages and disadvantages of traditional eating?

e) Which words do associate with healthy food?

II. Instruction

Listen to the passage carefully. You will have to write a suitable title.

The Passage

The twentieth century has brought with it many advances. With those advances, human lives have changed dramatically. In some ways life is worse, but mostly it is better. Changes in food preparation methods, for example, have improved our lives greatly.

The convenience of preparing food today is amazing. Even stoves have become too slow for us. Microwave cooking is much easier. We can press a few buttons and a meal is completely cooked in just a short time. People used to spend hours preparing an oven-cooked meal, and now they can use that time for other, better things. Plus, there are all kinds of portable, prepackaged foods we can buy. Heat them in the office microwave, and lunch at work is quick and easy.

Food preparation today allows for more variety. With refrigerators and freezers, we can preserve a lot of different foods in our homes. Since technology makes cooking so much faster, people are willing to make several dishes for even a small meal. Parents are more likely to let children be choosy, now that they can easily heat them up some prepackaged macaroni and cheese on the side. Needless to say, adults living in the same house may have very different eating habits as well. If they don't want to cook a lot of different dishes, it's common now to eat out at restaurants several times a week.

III. Recall and write the passage you have heard. You will have to complete it, within 30 minutes.

References

1. Marybeth Coleman (2002), using Quality Children's Literature to Increase Language minority Students' Reading Levels, retrieved from: http://gse.gmu.edu/assets/docs/lmtip/vol1/M.Coleman.doc
2. Craige (2008). 'Writing as a Way to Learn,' retrieved from:
3. *ibid.* cited from Craige (2008)
4. *ibid.* cited from Craige (2008)
5. Wallace C. Reading, OUP, 1992, 9-215.
6. Sharma PL. Evaluation and Counseling for Learners, Sarup and Sons, New Delhi, 2006, 215-234.
7. Spodek B. Teaching in the Early Years, Prentice Hall – Series in early childhood, 1972, 88-111.
8. *ibid.* 89p.
9. *ibid.* 90p.
10. Sharma PL. Evaluation and Counseling for Learners, Sarup and Sons, New Delhi, India, 2006, 215-234.
11. Ronald Mackay, Barkman B, Jordon RR. Reading in a Second Language, Newbury House Publishers, Rowley, Massachusetts, 1979, 187-198.
12. Patricia L. Some Issues in Studying the Role of Schemata, or Background Knowledge, in Second Language Comprehension, TESOL, 1983. Retrieved from.
13. Langer, Judith A. Writing to Study and Learn, 1986. Retrieved from.
14. Yael Bejarano. A Cooperative Small-Group Methodology in the Language Classroom, TESOL QUARTERLY, 1987; 21(3). Retrieved from.
15. James P Lantolf. Introducing Socio-cultural theory, 1994. Retrieved from.

16. Khaini Izwan Abdullah. Research in Reading and Writing: A Southeast Asian Collection,' Seameo Regional Language Centre, Singapore, 1994, 90-97.

17. *ibid.* 55-61.

18. *ibid.* 16-26.

19. Janice F Almasi, Margaret G Mckeown, Isabel L Beck. Twenty online resources on reading with comprehension and engagement,' Reading Online. 1996; 4(10). Retrieved from.

20. *ibid.* Dalton B, 2001.

21. Aek Phakit. Theoretical and Pedagogical Issues in ESL/EFL Teaching of Strategic Reading, TESOL. 2006; 1:19-50.

22. Chaudron. 2008. Retrieved from.

23. Craigie. Writing as a Way to Learn, 2008. Retrieved from.

24. Sing RK. English Language Teaching: Some Aspects Recollected, Book Enclave, Jaipur, India, 2008, 214p.

25. De Boer JJ, Dallman M. The Teaching of Reading, Holt Rinehart and Winston, Inc. New York, 1960, 117-130

26. Cathy Burnett, Julia Myers. Teaching English 3-11, Atlantic Publishers & Distributers, London, New York, 2004, 42-43.

27. *opcit.* Wallace C, 1998, 6-7.

28. Fieldhouse AE. How to Conduct a Reading Survey, OUP, 1957, 6-12.

29. Richard R Day. New Ways in Teaching Reading, TESOL series, Maryland USA, 1993, 9p.

30. Duffy GG, Sherman GB. Systematic Reading Instruction, Second Edition Harper and Row, New York, 1977, 32-33.

31. Retrieved from.

32. Retrieved from.

33. Retrieved from.

34. *opcit*. Duffy GG, Sherman GB. 1977, 13-15.

35. *opcit*. Sharma, 2006, 215p.

36. *opcit*. Deboer, Dallman, 1960, 117.

37. *opcit*. Sharma PL. 2006, 218-219.

38. Vernon MD. Backwardness in Reading—A study of its nature and origin, CUP, 1958, 1-117.

39. Oakhill J, Cain K. Reading Processes in Children, Encyclopedia of Language and Linguistics. 2006; 10:382p.

40. *Ibid*, 382p.

41. *Ibid*, 383p.

42. *Ibid,* 383p.

43. Retrieved from.

44. Retrieved from.

45. Zheng LIN (2002), retrieved from.

46. *ibid.* Zheng LIN (2002)

47. 43. *ibid.* Zheng LIN (2002)

48. 44. *ibid.* Zheng LIN (2002)

49. Retrieved from.

50. Retrieved from.

51. Retrieved from.

52. Paul Thomas Young. 'A study upon Recall of Pleasant and Unpleasant Words', The American Journal of Psychology, University of Illinois Press. 1937; 49(4):581-596. Retrieved from.

53. James W Aldridge, Michael T Farrel. 'Long-term Recency Effect in Free Recall,' American Journal of Psychology, University of Illinois Press. 1977; 90(3):475-479. retrieved from:

54. Langer Judith A. Writing to Study and Learn, 1986. Retrieved from.

55. Bohlmeyer, Elaine Morton. Others. Effects of Spontaneous and Imposed Study Strategies on Recall of Prose, Washington, D.C, 1987, Retrieved from.

56. Donald J Richgels *et al.* Awareness of Four Text Structures: Effects on

Recall of Expository Text, Reading Research Quarterly, Louisiana State University. 1987; 22(2):176-196.

57. Patricia L Carrel. Content and Formal Schemata in ESL Reading, TESOL quarterly. 1987; 21(3):461-481. Retrieved from.

58. Mark Sadoski, Zeba Quast. Reader Response and Long-term Recall for Journalistic Text: The Roles of Imagery, Affect, and Importance, Reading Research Quarterly, Louisiana State University. 1990; 25(4):256-271.

59. John Hammadou. Interrelationships among prior Knowledge, Inference, and Language Proficiency in Foreign Language Recall,'The Modern Language Journal. Blackwell Publishing. 1991; 75(1):27-38.

60. McDaniel, Mark A *et al.* Text Expectancy, Study Strategies and Recall of Prose, the American Educational Research Association, Chicago, 1991. Retrieved from.

61. Gabriel A Appel, James P Lantolf. Speaking as Mediation: A Study of L1 and L2 Text Recall Tasks, The Modern Language Journal Cornell University, Ithaca, 1994; 78(4):437-452.

62. Sue Barry, Alejandro A Lazarte. Embedded Clauses Effects on Recall: Does High Prior Knowledge of Content Domain Overcome Syntactic Complexity in Students of Spanish, The Modern Language Journal, Auburn University. 1995; 79(4):491-504.

63. Dorothy M Chun, Jan L Plass. Research on Text Comprehension in Multimedia Environments, Language Learning &Technology. 1997; 1(1):60-81. Retrieved from.

64. Oren Lamm. Two Case studies of poor spelling in Hebrew: the recognition and recall of words' root letters; John Wiley & Sons, Ltd. 1997; 3(4):201-221.

65. Farzad Sharifian. The Mnemonic influence of Self-cues on Narrative Recall, Issues in Educational Research. 2001; 11(1):15-24. Retrieved from.

66. Shagufta Imtiaz. Gender Differences in Recall in Expository Writing among School Children, Journal of the Linguistic Society of India, Pune. 2004; 65:59-74.

67. Patricia L Carrel. Awareness of Text Structure: Effects on Recall, Language Learning Research Club, the University of Akron. 2006; 42(1):1-18.

68. Yuh-Fang Chang. On the use of the immediate recall task as a measure of second language reading comprehension; Language Testing. 2006; 23(4):520-543. retrieved from:

69. Craigie. Writing as a Way to Learn, 2008. Retrieved from.

70. Carrel Patricia L. Content and Formal Schemata in ESL Reading, TESOL quarterly. 1987; 21(3):461-481.

71. Craige. Writing as a Way to Learn. Retrieved from, 2008.

72. Dalton B. Twenty online resources on reading with comprehension and engagement, Reading Online, Retrieved from. 2001; 4(10).

73. De Boer JJ, Dallman M. The Teaching of Reading, Holt Rinehart and Winston, Inc. New York, 1960, 117-130.

74. Donald J Richgels *et al.* Awareness of Four Text Structures: Effects on Recall of Expository Text, Reading Research Quarterly, Louisiana State University, 1987; 12(2):176-196.

75. Dorothy M Chun, Jan L Plass. Research on Text Comprehension in Multimedia Environments, Language Learning &Technology, July. 1997; 1(1):60-81.

76. Falk JS. Linguistics and Language—A survey of Basic Concepts and Implications, John Wiley and Sons, New York, 1978.

77. Farzad Sharifian. The Mnemonic influence of Self-cues on Narrative Recall,' Issues in Educational Research. 2001; 11(1):15-24.

78. Fieldhouse AE. How to Conduct a Reading Survey, OUP, 1957, 6-12.

79. Gabriel A Appel, James P Lantolf Speaking as Mediation: A Study of L1 and L2 Text Recall Tasks, the Modern Language Journal Cornell University, Ithaca. 1994; 78(4):437-452.

80. Gerald DG, Sherman GB. Systematic Reading Instruction, Second Edition Harper and Row, New York, 1977, 32-33.

81. James P Lantolf. Introducing Socio-cultural theory, 1994. Retrieved from.

82. James W Aldridge, Michael T Farrel. Long-term Recency Effect in Free Recall, American Journal of Psychology, University of Illinois Press. 1977; 90(3):475-479.

83. John Hammadou. Interrelationships among Prior Knowledge, Inference, and Language Proficiency in Foreign Language Recall, the

Modern Language Journal, Blackwell Publishing. 1991; 75(1):27-38.

84. Langer Judith A. Writing to Study and Learn, 1986. Retrieved from

85. Mark Sadoski, Zeba Quast. Reader Response and Long-term Recall for Journalistic Text: The Roles of Imagery, Affect, and Importance,' Reading Research Quarterly, Louisiana State University. 1990; 15(4):256-271.

86. McDaniel, Mark A., *et al.* Text Expectancy, Study Strategies and Recall of Prose, the American Educational Research Association, Chicago, 1991.

87. Marybeth Coleman. Using Quality Children's Literature to Increase Language minority Students Reading Levels, 2002. Retrieved from. http://gse.gmu.edu/assets/docs/lmtip/vol1/M.Coleman.doc

88. Oakhill J, Cain K. Reading Processes in Children, Encyclopedia of Language and Linguistics. 2006; 10:379-385.

89. Patricia L Carrel. Awareness of Text Structure: Effects on Recall, Language Learning Research Club, the University of Akron. 2006; 42(1):1-18.

90. Patricia L. Some Issues in Studying the Role of Schemata, or Background Knowledge, in Second Language Comprehension, TESOL, 1983.

91. Paul Thomas Young. A study upon Recall of Pleasant and Unpleasant Words, The American Journal of Psychology, University of Illinois Press. 1937; 49(4):581-596.

92. Phakit Aek. Theoretical and Pedagogical Issues in ESL/EFL Teaching of Strategic Reading, TESOL. 2006; 1:1950p.

93. Ronald Mackay, Barkman B, Jordon RR. Reading in a Second Language, Newbury House Publishers, Rowley, Massachusetts, 1979, 187-198.

94. Richard R Day. New Ways in Teaching Reading, TESOL series, Maryland USA, 1993, 9p.

95. Sharma PL. Evaluation and Counseling for Learners, Sarup and Sons, New Delhi, India, 2006, 215-234.

96. Shagufta Imtiaz. Gender Differences in Recall in Expository Writing among School Children, Journal of the Linguistic Society of India, Pune. 2004; 65:59-74.

97. Sing RK. English Language Teaching: Some Aspects Recollected, Book Enclave, Jaipur, India, 2008, 214p.

98. Spodek B. Teaching in the Early Years, Prentice Hall – Series in early childhood, 1972, 88-111.

99. Sue Barry, Alejandro A Lazarte. Embedded Clauses Effects on Recall: Does High Prior Knowledge of Content Domain Overcome Syntactic Complexity in Students of Spanish, The Modern Language Journal, Auburn University. 1995; 79(4):491-504.

100. Tickoo ML. Research in Reading and Writing: A Southeast Asian Collection, Seameo Regional Language Centre, Singapore, 1994, 90-97.

101. Vernon MD. Backwardness in Reading—A study of its nature and origin, CUP, 1958, 1-117.

102. Wallace C. Reading, OUP, 1992, 9-215.

103. Weaver C. Reading Process and Practice, Portsmouth, Heinemann Educational Books, 1988, 27p.

104. Yael Bejarano. A Cooperative Small-Group Methodology in the Language Classroom, TESOL QUARTERLY. 1987; 21:3.

Internet Links

- http://education.curtin.edu.au/iier/iier11/sharifian.html
- http://en.wikipedia.org/wiki/Top-down
- http://fds.oup.com/www.oup.com/pdf/elt/catalog/0-19-442160-0-a.pdf
- http://journals.comcambridge.org/action/displayAbstract?frompage=online&aid=2844296
- http://llt.msu.edu/vol1num1/chun_plass/
- http://rhetoric.sdsu.edu/lore/2_1/08_kang.pdf
- http://www.sil.org/Lingualinks/AuthorsMZ.htm#Walter
- http://www.reading.com.au/222/writing-as-a-way-to-learn
- http://www.majortests.com/sat/reading-comprehension.php
- http://www.en.wikipedia.org/wiki/Reading_comprehension.htm
- http://www.readingrockets.org/article/252.htm
- http://www.readingonline.org/editorial/edit_index.asp?HREF=/editorial/may2001/index.html

- http://www.time4learning.com/readingpyramid/Comprehension.htm
- http://www.alibris.com/search/books/qwork/6574274/used/Teaching%20Reading:%20A%20Global%20Approach
- http://www.jstor.org/action/showPublication?journalCode=amerjapsy.
- http://www.thefreedictionary.com/recall
- http://www.linkinghub.elsevier.com/retrieve/pii/S0346251X97000092
- www.eric.ed.gov/ERICWebPortal/recordDetail?accno=ED331871 - 30k
- www.eric.ed.gov/ERICWebPortal/recordDetail?accno=EJ16907528k-
- www.eric.ed.gov/ERICWebPortal/recordDetail?accno=ED215924-31K
- www.periodicos.ufsc.br/index.php/desterro/article/viewPDFInterstitial/9023/8360
- http://www.reading.com.au/222/writing-as-a-way-to-learn
- http://www.eric.ed.gov/ERICWebPortal/custom/portlets/recordDetails/detailmini.jsp?_nfpb=true&_&ERICExtSearch_SearchValue_0=ED297316&ERICExtSearch_SearchType_0=no&accno=ED297316
- www.periodicos.ufsc.br/index.php/desterro/article/viewPDFInterstitial/9023/8360
- http://www.linkinghub.elsevier.com/retrieve/pii/S0346251X97000092
- http://fds.oup.com/www.oup.com/pdf/elt/catalog/0-19-442160-0-a.pdf
- http://www.readingonline.org/editorial/edit_index.asp?HREF=/editorial/may2001/index.html
- http://journals.comcambridge.org/action/displayAbstract?frompage=online&aid=2844296
- http://www.reading.com.au/222/writing-as-a-way-to-learn
- http://www.time4learning.com/readingpyramid/Comprehension.htm
- http://www.majortests.com/sat/reading-comprehension.php
- http://www.en.wikipedia.org/wiki/Reading_comprehension.htm

- http://en.wikipedia.org/wiki/Top-down
- http://www.sil.org/Lingualinks/AuthorsMZ.htm#Walter
- http://www.sil.org/lingualinks/literacy/ReferenceMaterials/GlossaryOf LiteracyTerms/WhatIsReadingModel.htm
- http://www.readingrockets.org/article/252.htm
- http://www.alibris.com/search/books/qwork/6574274/used/Teaching%20Reading:%20A%20Global%20Approach
- www.eric.ed.gov/ERICWebPortal/recordDetail?accno=ED215924-31K
- http://www.jstor.org/action/showPublication?journalCode=amerjapsy.
- www.eric.ed.gov/ERICWebPortal/recordDetail?accno=EJ16907528k-
- http://www.eric.ed.gov/ERICWebPortal/custom/portlets/recordDetails/detailmini.jsp?_nfpb=true&_&ERICExtSearch_SearchValue_0=ED297316&ERICExtSearch_SearchType_0=no&accno=ED297316
- www.eric.ed.gov/ERICWebPortal/recordDetail?accno=ED282184
- http://rhetoric.sdsu.edu/lore/2_1/08_kang.pdf
- www.eric.ed.gov/ERICWebPortal/recordDetail?accno=ED331871 - 30k
- http://llt.msu.edu/vol1num1/chun_plass/
- http://www3.interscience.wiley.com/journal/15408/abstract?CRETRY=1&SRETRY=0
- http://education.curtin.edu.au/iier/iier11/sharifian.htm
- http://ltj.sagepub.com/cgi/content/abstract/23/4/520
- <http://www.reading.com.au/222/writing-as-a-way-to-learn
- http://www.reading.com.au/222/writing-as-a-way-to-learn
- http://www.readingonline.org/editorial/edit_index.asp?HREF=/editorial/may2001/index.html
- http://fds.oup.com/www.oup.com/pdf/elt/catalog/0-19-442160-0-a.pdf
- http://www.eric.ed.gov/ERICWebPortal/custom/portlets/recordDetails/detailmini.jsp?_nfpb=true&_&ERICExtSearch_SearchValue_0=ED297316&ERICExtSearch_SearchType_0=no&accno=ED297316